Maria Tallchief
The First Native American Ballerina

Biography of Famous People

Children's Biography Books

BABY PROFESSOR

EDUCATION KIDS

Speedy Publishing LLC

40 E. Main St. #1156

Newark, DE 19711

www.speedypublishing.com

Copyright 2017

Maria Tallchief was the first Native American ballerina. She was known for her role in *The Nutcracker* as the Sugarplum Fairy. She was born in Fairfax, Oklahoma on January 24, 1925. In this book, you will be learning about her life and talents, as well as learning about other well-known Native Americans.

HER FAMILY

Maria was born in 1925 on the Osage Indian Reservation in Fairfax, Oklahoma. Ruth Porter, her mother, was a Scots-Irish woman that loved dance and music. Her father was Alexander Tallchief, an Osage Indian that became wealthy from an oil discovery on the Osage land. Her family called her Betty Marie, even though she is known as Maria Tallchief.

Maria Tallchief

Maria liked to play outside with Marjorie, her sister, as they were growing up. Like her mother, she also enjoyed music and dancing. She learned to play the piano and practiced her dancing with a local dance instructor. Occasionally, her mother would permit Maria and Marjorie to watch the dancers and listen to the music as the Osage tribe would celebrate their culture secretly.

Marjorie also became a well-known ballerina and became the first Native American to earn the title of "premiere danseuse etoile", otherwise known as prima ballerina, for the Paris Opera Ballet.

In 1946, she was married to choreographer George Balanchine.

THEIR MOVE TO LOS ANGELES

Maria's family moved to Los Angeles, California when she was eight years old. She was mesmerized when she saw the Pacific Ocean. She started taking dance lessons right away at Mr. Belcher's School of Ballet.

Her days became quite busy. She would start early in the morning, practicing the piano for an hour prior to going to school. She would then practice the piano for another hour after school as well as attending ballet lessons. She enjoyed her time spent practicing both her dance and the piano.

CHOOSING DANCE

When Maria was twelve, her father made her decide between piano or dance. While it was a difficult decision, she decided to dance and started training at a different ballet school. Madame Nijinska, the famous Russian ballerina, was her new teacher.

For the following five years, she was a student of Madame Nijinska. She learned to dance with grace, emotion and power. She soon learned that being perfect was not enough, and that she had to dance and feel with the music.

Ballet Russe de Monte Carlo Poster

MOVING TO NEW YORK

It became Maria's dream to join the Ballet Russe de Monte Carlo. At the age of seventeen, she decided to pursue that dream and moved to New York. She soon became a member of this famous ballet company. They saw talent and she soon became a featured soloist.

She traveled around the world and danced in several of Europe's famous ballet houses. She became the first prima ballerina of the New York City Ballet in 1947.

In 1965, Maria retired from dancing and in 1981, along with her sister, founded the Chicago City Ballet.

She appears in "Ballet Russes", a 2005 award winning documentary about the "Ballet Russe de Monte Carlo dancers.

Maria Tallchief featured in Dance Magazine July 1961 cover

MARIA'S HONORS

She is considered by many to be one of the world's greatest dancers and has won several honors during her career. Listed below are just a few of her honors:

The Osage people named her Wa-Xthe-Thomba meaning "Woman of Two Worlds."

In 1996, she received the Kennedy Centers Honors award for her American culture lifetime contributions.

Maria Tallchief

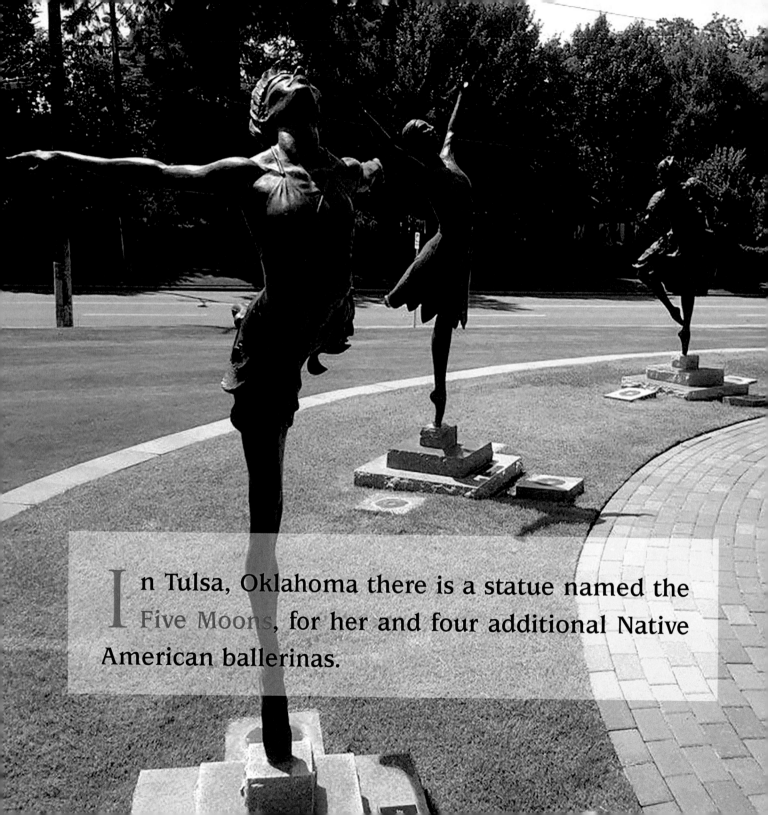

In Tulsa, Oklahoma there is a statue named the Five Moons, for her and four additional Native American ballerinas.

In 1999, she was awarded with the National Medal of Arts.

Pocahontas hugging her father

OTHER WELL-KNOWN NATIVE AMERICANS

Several Native American Indians have made a tremendous influence and impact on society. Read further to learn more about some of these famous people and great leaders.

SQUANTO (1581-1622)

S quanto (also known as Tisquantum) had an interesting life. When he was a teen, he met up with a group of Europeans that were led by Captain Weymouth. He then learned to speak English and traveled to England with them. He soon became homesick and eventually returned to his homeland.

Statue of Squanto

He would not stay there long, however, and along with 19 other tribe members, was taken captive by Captain Weymouth, returned to Europe, and the sold as slaves. Several years

later, he again found his way home, but when he arrived, he found that all of his village had passed away from disease. He joined another tribe and remained with them.

The Pilgrims arrived about a year later and proceeded to settle in Plymouth close to Squanto's tribe. Since he was able to speak English, he helped in establishing a treaty between the Pilgrims and the local Native American peoples. He also taught the Pilgrims to learning to grow local crops, catch fish, and how to survive the winters. More than likely, the Pilgrims would not have survived without his help. In spite of everything bad that had happened to him, Squanto still hoped for peace and wanted to help others.

Pocahontas

POCAHONTAS (1595-1617)

Pocahontas was born the daughter of the Powhatan tribe chief, living close to the English settlement in Jamestown, Virginia. She saved Captain John Smith, the Jamestown leader, when he visited their village. In addition, she helped in warning settlers of an attack by her father and his warriors.

She was later captured and the settlers held her for ransom. They treated her well and she soon fell in love with John Rolfe, an English settler. After she married Rolfe, she returned to England with him and became a well-known celebrity. She unfortunately died at the young age of 22 in England.

Sequoyah

SEQUOYAH (1767-1843)

Sequoyah was a Cherokee tribe member. He created the Cherokee alphabet as well as a way in which to write the Cherokee language. He did this remarkable accomplishment all on his own. This was one of few times that a member of a pre-literate people created a writing system that was original and effective.

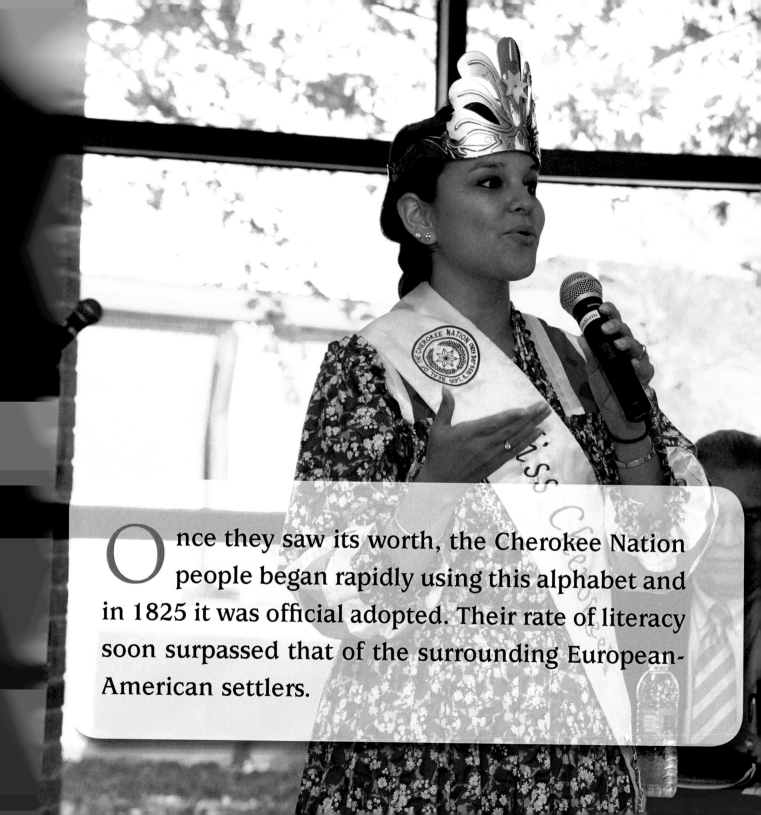

Once they saw its worth, the Cherokee Nation people began rapidly using this alphabet and in 1825 it was official adopted. Their rate of literacy soon surpassed that of the surrounding European-American settlers.

Black Hawk

BLACK HAWK (1767-1838)

He was known as a fierce and capable war Chief. Black Hawk commanded the Sauk tribes with the British during the War of 1812. He then fought in saving people's land from the settlers. Eventually he was captured and his people then lost their lands.

SACAJAWEA (1788-1812)

She was a Shoshone Indian tribe member. As a young girl, she became a slave once her village was attacked. She was later sold to Charbonneau, a French trapper, who then married her. When the famous explorers Lewis and Clark arrived, she was living with Charbonneau. They asked her to travel along with them to assist in translating with the Shoshone. She then joined them with their expedition and would play a key role in their successful travels to the Pacific Ocean.

Sacajawea, Lewis and Clark at Three Forks

Geronimo

GERONIMO (1829-1909)

He was the Chiricahua Apache tribe leader, leading the Apache in intense resistance for several years against invaders from both the west and from Mexico. His translated name is "one who yawns".

As a prominent medicine man and leader of the Bedonkohe band of Chiricahua Apache tribe, from 1850 to 1886 he joined with three other Chiricahua Apache bands – the Nednhi, the Chokonen, and the Chihenne – to perform several raids, including resistance to Mexican and US

Apache settlement in Arizona

military campaigns, as well as the territories of New Mexico and Arizona. These raids and the related combat actions were part of the Apache-United States conflict, which began with the American settlement in the Apache lands after the end of the war with Mexico in 1848.

Sitting Bull

SITTING BULL
(1831-1890)

Sitting Bull was well known for being the leader of the Lakota Sioux Plains Indians, and mostly known for his premonition that the Sioux would be victorious in a battle against the white man. He then proceeded to lead a group of warriors from the Arapahoe, Cheyenne, and Lakota tribes in battle which became known as the Battle of Little Big Horn fought against General Custer. During this battle, often referred to as Custer's Last Stand, he destroyed Custer's army completely, killing all of Custer's men.

JIM THORPE
(1888 - 1953)

Thorpe was raised in Oklahoma in the Sac and Fox Nation and is considered to be one of the best athletes ever. He played professional football, baseball and basketball. In addition, at the 1912 Olympics he won Gold Medals in the decathlon and pentathlon events.

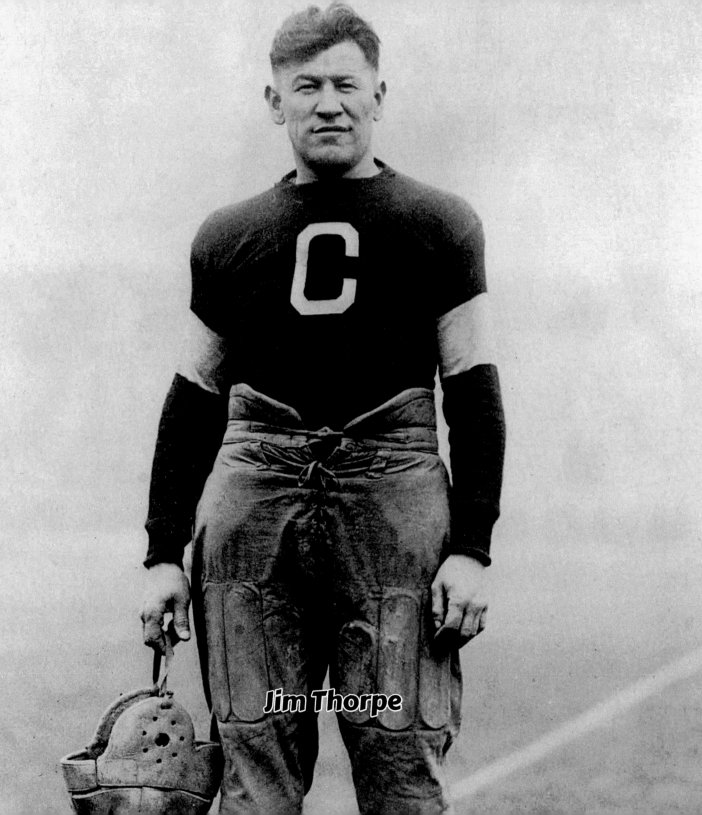
Jim Thorpe

Crazy Horse

CRAZY HORSE
(1840 – 1877)

Crazy Horse was a war leader of Oglala Lakota. He took arms up against Federal Government of the United States to fight against the encroachments on territories and the Lakota peoples' way of life, which included acting as decoy during the Fetterman Massacre as well as leading the war party victorious in June of 1876 at the Battle of the Little Bighorn.

Tecumseh

Other well-known Native Americans include Chief Joseph, Crazy Horse, Pontiac, Will Rogers, Cochise, Tecumseh, Hiawatha, Cochise and Red Cloud.

Pontiac

N ative Americans have played an important role in the history of the United States. These are just a few of the people that made a difference for their people.

For additional information about Native Americans you can go to your local library, research the internet, and ask questions of your teachers, family and friends.

Made in the USA
San Bernardino, CA
18 January 2018